S0-BUB-522

Dearest Sis Elizabeth,

For You To Always Remember

How Special You Are To Me

And To The World!

Love, Dan

YOU MATTER

It isn't just one thing...

It's everything. It's all the things you are—your heart, your mind, the way you interact with others—that mean so much. It's easy to see how much better the world is because of the way you spend your time, share your talents, and give the best of who you are.

Everywhere you go, and with all that you do, you make a difference...

YOU'RE
AMAZING.

Thank you.

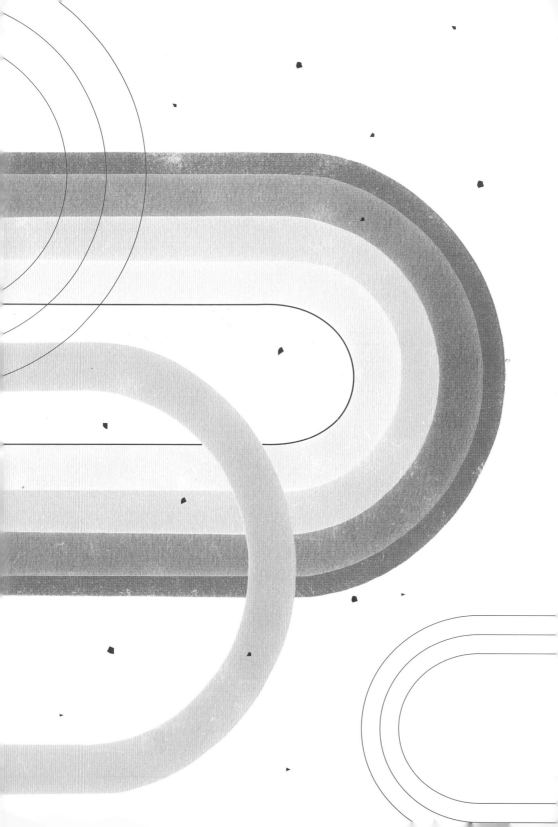

IF YOU COULD ONLY SENSE HOW
IMPORTANT YOU ARE TO
THE LIVES OF THOSE YOU MEET...

Fred Rogers

YOUR

kindness

MATTERS

THE WORK OF YOUR HEART,
THE WORK OF TAKING TIME,
TO LISTEN, TO HELP, IS
ALSO YOUR GIFT TO THE
WHOLE OF THE WORLD.

Jack Kornfield

You are not only good yourself,
but the cause of goodness in others.

SOCRATES

...give to the world the best
that you have, and the best
will come back to you.

MADELINE BRIDGES

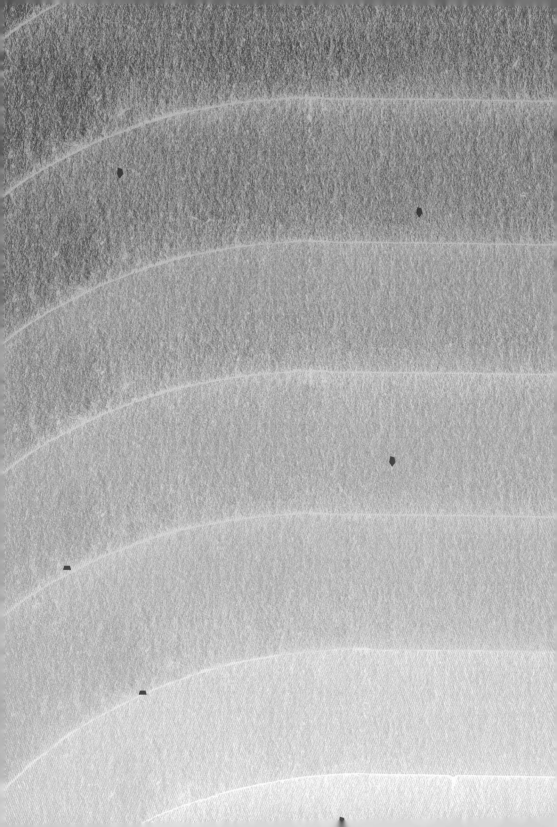

YOUR
spirit
MATTERS

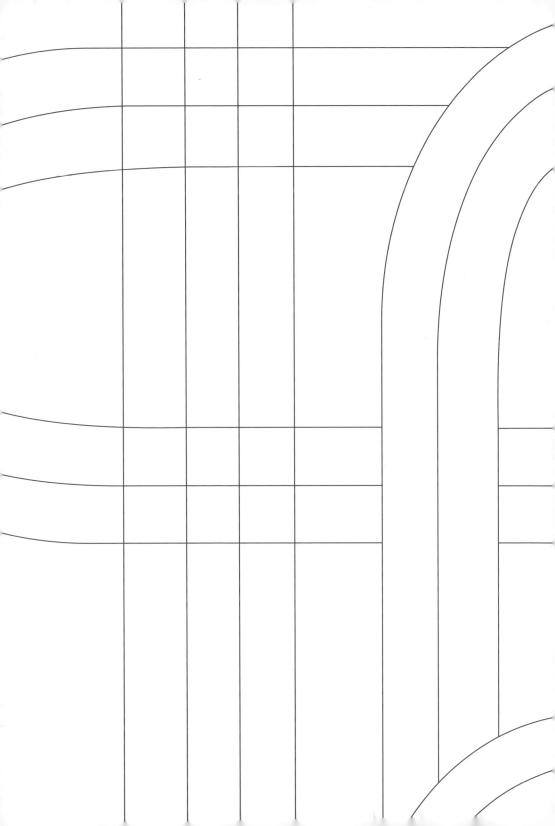

There is a force in the universe, which,
if we permit it, will flow through
us and produce miraculous results.

MAHATMA GANDHI

LET NOTHING DIM THE LIGHT THAT SHINES FROM WITHIN.

Maya Angelou

...YOU WERE MADE FOR AMAZING THINGS.

Josh Hinds

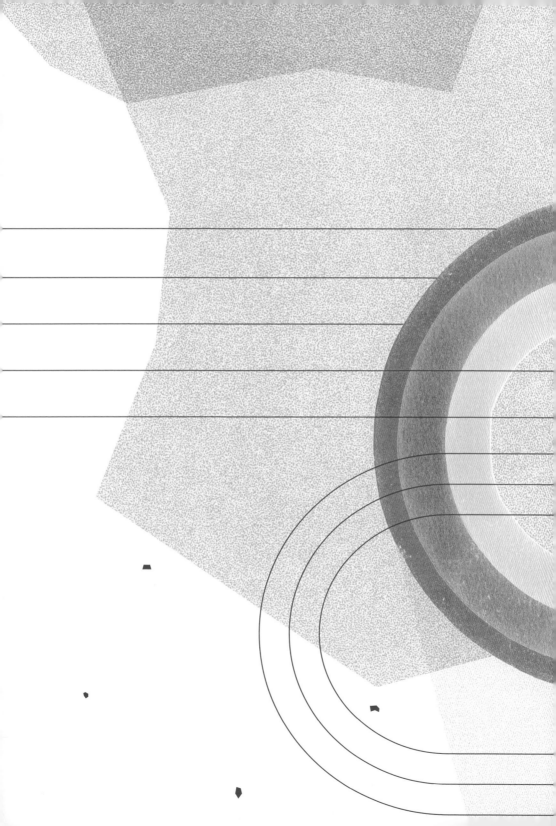

YOUR ideas MATTER

...YOU HAVE INFINITE POTENTIAL.
YOU CAN DO ANYTHING, MAKE
ANYTHING, DREAM ANYTHING.

Neil Gaiman

Because you are alive,
everything is possible.

THICH NHAT HANH

Realize how good you really are.

OG MANDINO

YOUR passion MATTERS

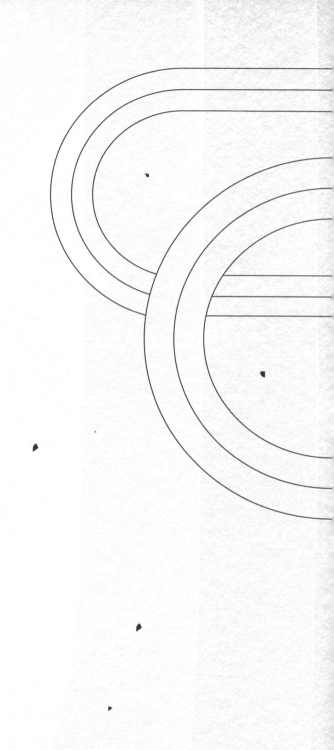

THINK OF THE WORLD YOU
CARRY INSIDE YOU.

Rainer Maria Rilke

You are everything you choose to be.
You are as unlimited as the endless universe.

SHAD HELMSTETTER

It is our privilege and
our adventure to discover
our own special light.

EVELYN DUNBAR

YOUR

uniqueness

MATTERS

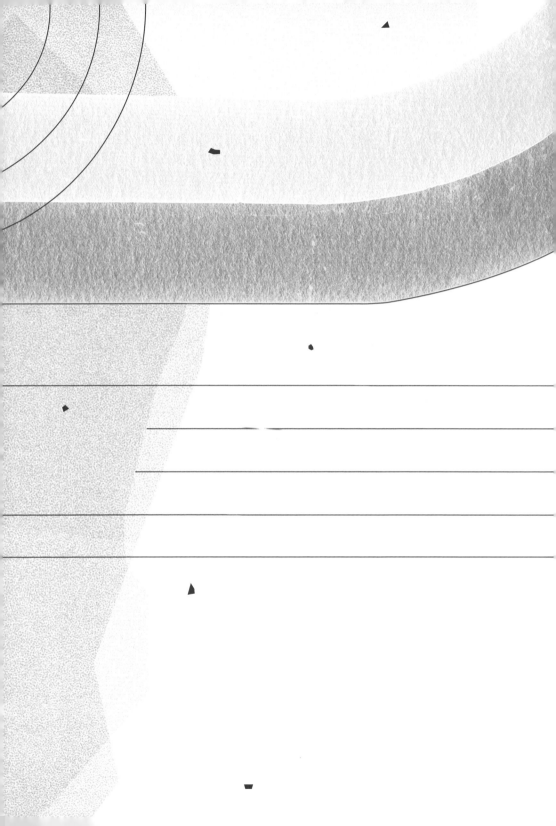

BY BEING YOURSELF, YOU
PUT SOMETHING WONDERFUL
INTO THE WORLD THAT WAS
NOT THERE BEFORE.

Edwin Elliot

NEVER BEFORE, SINCE THE
BEGINNING OF TIME, HAS
THERE EVER BEEN ANYBODY
EXACTLY LIKE YOU; AND
NEVER AGAIN THROUGHOUT
ALL THE AGES TO COME WILL
THERE EVER BE ANYBODY
EXACTLY LIKE YOU AGAIN.

Dale Carnegie

Don't look for miracles.
You yourself are the miracle.

HENRY MILLER

your generosity MATTERS

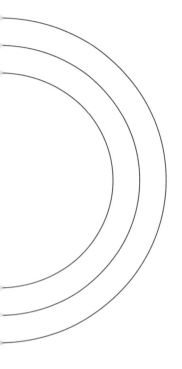

Real strength is not just a condition of one's muscle, but a tenderness in one's spirit.

MCCALLISTER DODDS

GUARD WELL WITHIN YOURSELF

THAT TREASURE, KINDNESS....

George Sand

Good people increase the
value of every other person...

KELLY ANN ROTHAUS

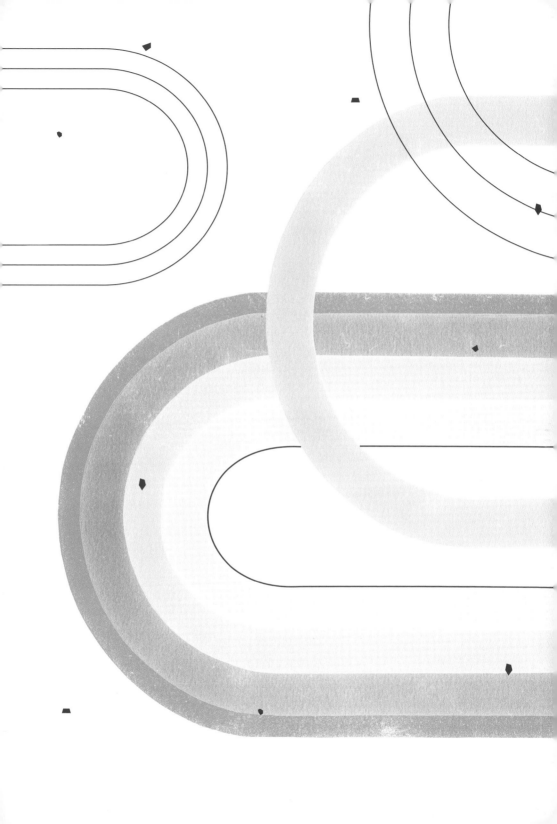

YOUR choices MATTER

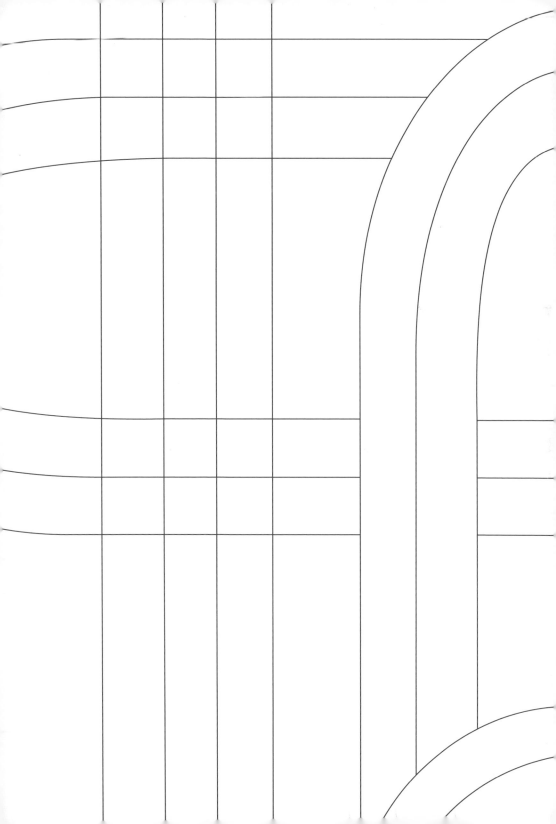

ACT AS IF WHAT YOU DO MAKES

A DIFFERENCE. IT DOES.

William James

A good head and a good heart are
always a formidable combination.

NELSON MANDELA

...THE WORLD NEEDS HUNDREDS OF THOUSANDS MORE PEOPLE LIKE YOU.

Evette Carter

YOUR **heart** MATTERS

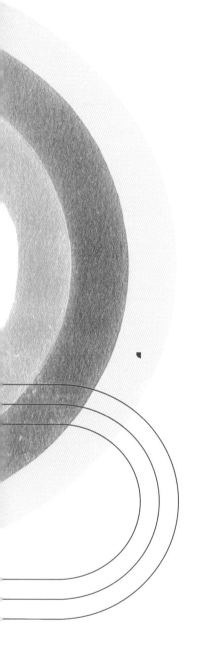

...what is done in love is done well.

VINCENT VAN GOGH

SOME PEOPLE ADD SO MUCH
BEAUTY TO BEING HUMAN.

Kobi Yamada

Your gifts matter. Your story matters.
Your dreams matter.

MICHAEL OHER

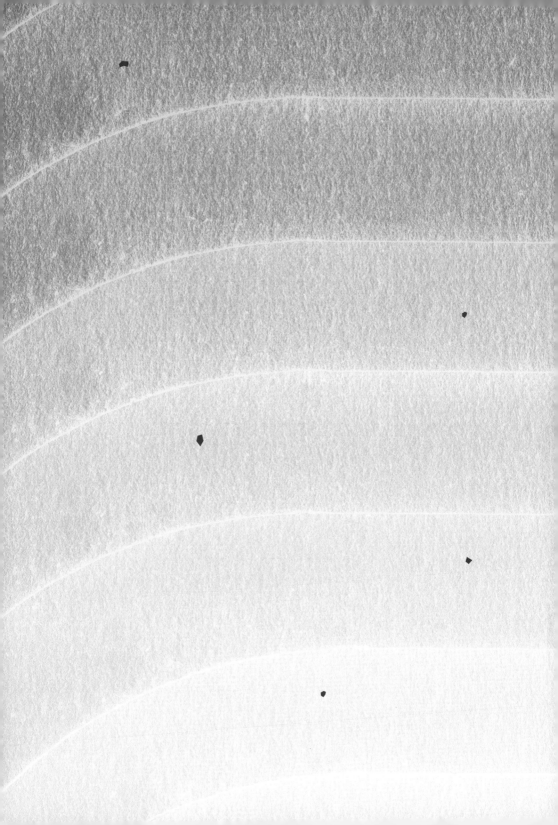

COMPENDIUM.
live inspired

Written and Compiled by: Amelia Riedler
Designed by: Jill Labieniec
Edited by: Cindy Wetterlund

Library of Congress Control Number: 2019958006 | ISBN: 978-1-970147-22-3

© 2021 by Compendium, Inc. All rights reserved. No part of this publication may be reproduced or transmitted in any form or by any means, electronic or mechanical, including photocopy, recording, or any storage and retrieval system now known or to be invented without written permission from the publisher. Contact: Compendium, Inc., 2815 Eastlake Avenue East, Suite 200, Seattle, WA 98102. You Matter; Compendium; live inspired; and the format, design, layout, and coloring used in this book are trademarks and/or trade dress of Compendium, Inc. This book may be ordered directly from the publisher, but please try your local bookstore first. Call us at 800.91.IDEAS, or come see our full line of inspiring products at live-inspired.com.

1st printing. Printed in China with soy and metallic inks on FSC®-Mix certified paper.

CONNECT WITH US
live-inspired.com | sayhello@compendiuminc.com

@compendiumliveinspired
#compendiumliveinspired

*Create
meaningful
moments
with gifts
that inspire.*